BLUFF YOUR WAY
IN
OPERA

PETER GAMMOND

RAVETTE BOOKS

Published by Ravette Books Limited
3 Glenside Estate, Star Road
Partridge Green, Horsham,
West Sussex RH13 8RA
(0403) 710392

First printed 1989
Reprinted 1991

Series Editor – Anne Tauté

Cover design – Jim Wire
Typesetting – System Graphics Ltd.
Printing & binding – Cox & Wyman Ltd.
Production – Oval Projects Ltd.

The Bluffer's Guides are based on
an original idea by Peter Wolfe.

For the Opera glasses on the cover
grateful thanks are extended to:
Universal Automatic Delivery,
Walmer, Nr. Deal, Kent.

We are indebted to Christopher Webber
for the denizens of the Operatic World
(p 13/14), Death Notes (p 58) and sundry
hints.

CONTENTS

Composers

INTRODUCTION

In opera, the bluffer will be moving in a world where bluffing is rampant, so there is clearly a need to choose the line of approach most carefully.

Ingrained cynicism seems to be the prevailing viewpoint. Opera is generally seen as an un-natural view of the world illogically set to music; unreality made even more unreal; in fact, little more than a lot of people with nothing much to sing about, all singing away like mad.

Though you may secretly concur with this view, which is one preponderantly held by the critical fraternity, a better line to take might be one of unswerving belief and admiration. You will find many of the paying operatic faithful taking the same view with scarcely a flicker of the eyelid. But you must, of course, be very careful because someone you have taken for an opera fan might well be just another bluffer in action. If you suspect this, simply out-manoeuvre them by going to extremes of operatic devotion, such as:

a) finding *Pelléas et Mélisande* brightly tuneful
b) assuming a bland understanding of the plot of whatever you happen to be listening to
c) expressing a firm belief that any singer you care to choose is a brilliant actor.

In many ways opera bluffing is not quite as simple as bluffing elsewhere, for example in the worlds of music in general or jazz, or in such adjacent zones of human philosophy as sex, religion or cricket. To bluff successfully in the opera world you should appear to have a minimal command of certain foreign languages; preferably Italian, though German will do. As opera was invented in Italy most of its essential terms are naturally couched in that language. But a spattering of the language and a convincing Italian accent can soon be acquired by visiting any of the numerous spaghetti houses that dot the globe; effectively supplemented in action by an expressively energetic use of the hands. The Italians always appreciate a good gesture.

Basic terms like 'bravo' ('that was a brave attempt'), 'bravissimo' ('that was an incredibly brave attempt') and 'magnifico' ('that was just about all right') will soon come naturally to the tongue.

Fortunately most of the operatic categories and terms are self-explanatory and readily translatable. The same applies to most Italian and French opera titles which are mainly the names of the work's principal character, for example – *Les Huguenots*. Even German should cause no particular terrors as most German words are similarly derived; though there are always one or two less obvious ones that you should be prepared for such as *Die Frau ohne Schatten* (*The Constipated Lady*).

The names of operas should generally be spoken in the original language unless it is too obvious what they mean and familiarity has bred suitable contempt – e.g. *The Magic Flute*, *The Marriage of Figaro* and *The Barber of Seville*. It shows a true familiarity with the opera repertoire if you abbreviate these to *The Flute*, *The Marriage* and *The Barber*. Similarly with other popular titles like *Cavalleria Rusticana* familiarly known as *Cav*; *I Pagliacci* (*Pag*); and others too obvious to explain such as *Trov*; *Trav*; and *Tris*.

Sweep away, with disdain, any arguments in favour of having opera in English merely for the sake of such advantages as being able to understand what is going on and knowing where to laugh. The true opera buff is staunchly for opera in the original language knowing full well that it is likely to be twice as tedious to know what is going on as not to know. Decide on a few obvious points for the intrusion of a sly laugh or a knowing smile and you will soon be regarded as an expert.

SOME BASIC DEFINITIONS

Opera was once defined (by Ambrose Bierce) as 'A play representing life in another world, whose inhabitants have no speech but song, no motions but gestures and no postures but attitudes'. There seems to be little that needs adding to that, except to classify the various kinds of opera that are available.

Merely to refer to all operas baldly as operas shows a clear lack of discernment. Bluffers must categorise as follows:

Grand Opera – A term obviously originated in Yorkshire, now slightly out of fashion, but suggestive of that which is heavily pretentious, unremittingly serious and generally to be avoided. The operas of Meyerbeer were decidedly grand and are consequently not much heard nowadays.

Opera seria – An Italian name for a particular brand of 18th century grand opera which dwelt with even greater seriousness on mythological or heroic subjects and usually lasted for a very long time. A sort of early Italian soap opera which, ideally, would have been presented in many parts in between the commercials. Hence 'seria', an Italian serial with no ending.

Opéra-comique – A special kind of French opera prevalent in the 19th century which was rarely the least bit comical. It was opera that was intended for the theatre known as l'Opéra-Comique rather than the austerely grand l'Opéra and was frequently lightened by the absence of *recitative* and helped along by a bit of spoken dialogue. A sly move toward the musical. Opéra-comique should never be translated as 'comic opera'; that is the role of:

7

Opéra-bouffe (French) or **opera buffa** (Italian) which are meant to be funny although it is not all that easy to differentiate between them and the general run of operas that are not meant to be funny.

Operetta – Originally a little or small opera but later supplanting the bouffe and buffa varieties as a lighter variety with spoken dialogue and plenty of good tunes intended for the ticket-buying section of the public whose boredom threshhold did not fit them to be true opera buffs. The English, just to confuse matters, called it comic opera or G & S (gay and silly), or later 'musical comedy', a type of entertainment that was frequently lacking in comedy or even music, in the purest sense.

There is no getting away from the fact that *true* opera is an entirely sung affair; and even where the extra platitudinous nature of the goings-on demands that things are pushed along a bit it must remain at least half sung in a manner that is known as *recitative* (from the Italian 'recitativo').

You will recognize these bits when the singer ceases to outpour in song and resorts to a sort of gabbled half-spoken chunk of music that could probably be bought from any respectable music-dealer at 50 pence a yard and which consequently sounds exactly the same in whatever opera and whatever language. It is usually accompanied by randomly interspersed chords on a harpsichord or whatever is available. Even the most dedicated opera fans are prone to admit that 'Why is your friend so late?', 'He must have missed the number 11 bus; they do run very infrequently and irregularly nowadays', 'Oh, dear!' might be capable of having more dramatic edge given to it by being spoken.

The Beginnings

The ancient Greeks are usually blamed for thinking up the idea in the first place. Having time to spare in between the occasional skirmish, and being used to long-windedness and incomprehensibilty, opera came to them naturally. In fact, nobody seems to know exactly how far the Greeks went, beyond singing or intoning some of their choruses, but there is a general belief that, as in all things, they went a bit farther than was absolutely necessary.

The true beginnings of opera, as we know it, happened in the houses of a couple of Florentine impresarios, Giovanni de' Bardi and Jacopi Corsi (later of Bardi & Corsi Ltd) who used to organise gatherings of musicians and poets in the hopes that some of them would come up with something or other. They had heard about the ancient Greek goings-on and hit upon the idea of reviving sung drama. They ignored such pointed questions as 'Why?' and 'What for?' and 'Have you gone mad?'

When asked what they would call this loony idea of people singing everything they could only suggest 'le musicale', having been drained of their creative powers by thinking it up in the first place. It wasn't until much later that someone chose 'opera', because it didn't really mean anything except 'a work' (as in opus) and was therefore suitably loose.

The first of the composers on the books of Bardi & Corsi to write an actual opera was one **Jacopo Peri** who knocked out a little piece called *Dafne* in 1597. (The score for this disappeared for many years until it was rediscovered by Richard Strauss and performed under his name in 1938.) It was, in spite of the resistance put up by the critics of the period, a modest success, while Peri's next musical, *Euridice* in 1600, scored a genuine run of 195 performances, including matinées, and it is still occasionally revived.

The first big name in opera was **Claudio Monteverdi** who made his mark with *La Favola d'Orfeo* in 1607 and then had two big commercial hits with *Il Ritorno d'Ulisse* (1641) and *L'Incoronazione di Poppea* (1642). All produced by the same old firm now operating as Bardi, Corsi & Gubby. Contrary to the beliefs of all but Giovanni and Jacopi, opera really caught on with audiences who seemed to like the idea of an entertainment that they were not expected to understand.

Further History

Italian opera was not only a top seller in Italy but rapidly took over the opera houses in every other country and, to the chagrin of the native composers, completely pushed out any indigenous attempts. The trouble was that, being on to a good thing, the Italians didn't feel greatly inclined to alter the model. Composers like Stradella and Vivaldi and Alessandro Scarlatti turned out neatly indistinguishable pieces full of *arias di bravura* and vast areas de *cantabile* surrounded by acres of *recitativo*, with much of the music written to suit the requirements of the all-powerful singers of the day.

It was not long, however, before the offices of Bardi & Corsi, etc. were shaken to their insubstantial foundations by foreigners starting to write their own operas. They were even forced to the lengths of employing a certain Salieri to go around the capitals of Europe and bump off the rising opposition.

The Italians didn't mind all that much because they were still writing plenty of operas of their own, with fellows like Rossini and Donizetti competing to see who could write an opera in the shortest possible time.

It was Mozart who started the Germans off with the

idea that they could write opera just as well as a lot of Italians; and irritatingly proved it by writing five or six imperishable classics. Bluffers should hold him indirectly responsible for Wagner. In between came people like Weber who made magic and fairies respectable subjects for opera by writing *Der Freischütz* and *Oberon*. One of his pupils was Meyerbeer who proceeded to carry opera to the extremes of grandeur and was very successful in his day. As in many other things like politics and war, the Germans saw no reason why opera should be restricted in any way. The bigger and noisier the better. The names of Richard I (Wagner) and Richard II (Strauss) should be declared the obvious exponents of this form.

The French took a different view. They went for lyrical sweetness and sexy drama. Ever resentful of any invasion of their culture, they did their best to resist the Wagnerian influence, but only partly succeeded. One of their biggest names was Massenet who probably has claims to be considered the most forgettable operatic composer of all time, apart from the Meditation from *Thais*. And apart, of course, from all those thousands of opera composers who are forgotten completely. There are regular expensive attempts to revive him which all end up with shelves full of unbought scores or recordings. Later came such innovators as Berlioz, Debussy and Ravel who continued to prove that the French had no answer to Puccini. Spanish opera is similar to the French with castanets added.

British operatic history is a boon to the bluffer, being brief and undemanding. There was Purcell who wrote *The Fairy Queen* and, after a considerable gap, Britten who re-wrote it, along with some very individual works of his own.

In between came Handel (a German who wrote Italian operas and filled the London theatres with them); *The Beggar's Opera*, a collection of second-hand folksongs with

11

rude dialogue in between (a category known as ballad opera – hardly an opera at all, really) only leading the way to Gilbert & Sullivan; Rutland Boughton; Delius (who wrote an opera about a firm of building contractors called *Fennimore & Gerda*); and Dame Ethel Smyth who proved that women couldn't write operas just as well as men.

The Americans had an international success with *Porgy and Bess*.

The world operatic map is very similar to the present day political one. It too has a sort of iron curtain. To the west is the capitalist world of Italian-based opera written for the rich and the intellectual, with a few left-wing deviants. To the east is the world of mainly peasant opera with a few right-wing deviants. Eastern European opera is either full of people wearing furry hats, dancing athletic dances on their haunches and swinging wildly from moods of drunken hilarity to bleak depression; or it is mythological and full of gnomes. The West has quite taken to a few of them, translated into English, like *The Bartered Bride* from Czechoslovakia; or *Prince Igor*, *Eugene Onegin* and *Coq d'Or* from Russia.

The bluffer will unquestionably find a fertile field for his imaginative quests in such areas as Rumania, Albania or Westphalia.

By 1910 a compilation (by Towers) listed 28,015 operas; and composers have been writing them ever since.

THE OPERATIC WORLD

The operatic world is remarkably similar to the religious. Its foundation is an act of unprovable faith; an unswerving belief that opera works on behalf of the devout even in the face of continual disaster. The main difference between opera and the Church is that the opera collection is made first.

The operatic religion is split up into many sects dominated by the Catholic Italian and the Lutherian German schools. It is worshipped in many elaborate temples: Il Teatro Communale (Florence), Covent Garden (London), La Scala (Milan), San Carlo (Naples), La Fenice (Venice), L'Opéra (Paris), The Met (New York), Liceo (Barcelona), Teatro Dell'Opera (Rome) on the one hand; Das Festspielhaus (Bayreuth), Die Deutsche Staatsoper (East Berlin), Die Deutsche Oper (West Berlin), The Kirov (Leningrad), The Bolshoi (Moscow), Das Hof und National (Munich), The National (Prague), etc., on the other. Some, like Die Staatsoper in Vienna are literally the centre of the city, where everyone meets and round which life revolves. No matter how tatty and hackneyed the productions within, the congregation will faithfully attend all services. Then there are new places like the Opera House in Sydney where, as with the Barbican in London, people are still trying to find a way in.

The operatic world is run by a vast hierarchy of art and business interests; inhabiting many offices, with an edifice of administrators, directors and managers:

General Manager/Director: called Intendant abroad, whose job it is to get hold of enough cash to pay the hordes of people involved in a production. As opera becomes more difficult to finance, they are less given to megalomania than they used to be. They are conscientious, aristocratic of bearing, immaculate of dress, and get ulcers.

Musical Director: sets the company tone. Can be:
a)   young, energetic and ambitious, or
b)   elderly, placid and serene.
The latter are the greater tyrants, and rule with a baton of iron.

Music Staff: Players (80 or so) collectively called The Band. Feel opera to be beneath them, though behaviour has improved since the invention of the synthesiser. Assistant conductors do the donkey work of rehearsal, and get to conduct revivals of old productions. Repetiteurs (lit. 'repeaters') are overworked pianists who note-bash for individual singers and at production rehearsals. Ashen-faced, they develop a technique for playing in their sleep.

Chorus: about 80 or so, they divide equally between sopranos (knitters), mezzos (flirts), tenors (poker players) and basses (real ale men). One Big Happy Family, so are given minders (Chorus Masters) to stop fights when they're depressed and argumentative.

Producer: equivalent of director in films. Unless the producer is East German (or called Sir or Dr) singers treat them with suspicion. Most home-products are Oxbridge, smart and very, very sensitive. They can be found plotting in Thai restaurants with:

Designers: the genii of the stage, creating magic from nothing (budget of £250,000), demanding little but artistic satisfaction (£20,000 to make models of the set). They also deal with costumes and lighting and may be specialists in one or the other. Laura Ashley look (men); black leather (women). Laid-back, long-suffering and amused. Amused because the actual work is done by experts like **Stage Carpenters.**

There are also hangers-on like:

- **movement groups** (tall, squat or arthritic ballet dancers)
- **extras** ('resting' actors disguised as peasantry, spear-carriers, and processions of cardinals)
- **sword-swallowers** and other circus artistes (for *The Bartered Bride*)
- **critics**.

Opera Critics and Historians

Opera critics are like all other critics, but worse. They are either wizened or short-sighted and many have foreign accents, even if they come from Bolton. You can spot them at the opera because they are the the ones who are not applauding or shouting 'bravo' and they sit at the ends of rows in order to escape at the first possible opportunity, ostensibly to get their copy written, but really to get to the bar.

Nothing is ever right for opera critics. Notable for taking the opposite view from the opera public, who are equally notable for being entirely uncritical, they have a vision of some perfect production short of which all actual productions lamentably fall. This perfect production would naturally utilize their immaculate talents as sole director with unlimited choice of performers and unlimited cash.

Opera critics take the view that each succeeding production by somebody else of a given work is slightly worse than the one before. The one they liked was in some distant opera house many years ago and this has not since been bettered. The singer of today cannot, of course, even begin to equal the great so-and-so; their top notes are lower and less effective, likewise their acting. Whatever the producer under review has conceived is ill-done. The fact that it is highly effective and is sending the audience into raptures leaves an opera critic unmoved. Something, or even everything, is deviating from his preconception of the work.

Of course, if he is allowed to go on long enough, he will be saying just the same about some future performance in contrast with the present one; which, by then, will have become yet another mellow memory.

Opera historians are more or less the same, with the same inclinations, but even more so.

Audiences and Opera Lovers

Opera audiences, in contrast to opera critics, are mainly uncritical. This is not to say that they are lacking in appreciation of the finer points of operatic performance or are totally oblivious of the golden tonsils of the past, but that they have come to the opera to enjoy themselves. Unlike the critics, they have had to pay for their seats and, in spite of the subsidy, have had to pay rather a lot. They are not going to splash out in order to have a good moan. They have come to see Domingo or Kanawa, and they have come to see *La Traviata*, or whatever, and even if it turns out to be one of opera's frequent disasters, they are going to cheer like mad at the end and create a triumph that will go down in the annals of opera, where the triumph will be written up by the aforementioned critic after a good bottle of wine, and immortalised as that great day in the year dot when so and so sang such and such as it had never been sung before.

Opera audiences tend to like to dress up to do justice to the chandeliers and the champagne in the crush bar. A lot of people go to the opera nowadays dressed in jeans and open necked shirts, and so forth, but they are kept in the back seats.

A typically English opera experience is Glyndebourne –

that is if one can get a ticket. But it is simple to bluff that you've been there. Assume that a car with its load of uncomfortable people in evening dress, a hamper of food and a crate of champers, is departing from London or thereabouts, in the afternoon (it is advisable to set off down the A23 with two or maybe three hours to spare). The party passes in uproarious mood through Godstone, East Grinstead, Wych Cross, bearing left to Uckfield and moving down the A26 and passing, in spite of protests from certain members, the Cock Inn, on the way to Ringmer and Glyndebourne. Of course, some may prefer to go by Sanderstead, Warlingham, Oxted, Edenbridge, Hartfield and Maresfield to fully enjoy the Ashdown Forest and the South Downs. There may even be those who like the Blindley Heath, Crawley Down, Turners Hill, Ardingley, Lindfield, Scaynes Hill and Chailey route, but these are mainly eccentrics and tend to get lost either at Newick Green or Barcombe Mills. If you end up in Brighton, there is a bus from there.

In any case, whichever route is taken, most parties get stuck in a traffic jam, near Lewes, where they should never have been in the first place.

Remember that, being England, the highlight of the evening, the picnic on the lawn in the long interval, will end up with the party avoiding the rain in the back of the car in the carpark or huddled in a dripping marquee. Having bought a large and expensive programme and a small and expensive drink and tried to scrape the mud off the evening dress, the traveller may well miss most of the opera as no-one is allowed in after the overture has begun. The opera is, in any case, a minor part of the proceedings. The main thing is to observe who is there. After they have returned safely home via (etc., etc.) they will all tell their jealous friends what a wonderful time they had. It's quite a good gimmick to say "I didn't bother to go this year" – and leave it at that.

SINGERS

Opera singers have their fair share of genius (a product always in short supply at the best of times), namely the ability to sing and execute a trill or two. The problem is they are required to act as well. Occasionally, they are endowed with both talents, but this is quite a rare event; and most of those so favoured seem to have decided to make a living in other related spheres of activity like the Church, politics or auctioneering.

Bluffers must be charitable, for it is difficult to see how someone fully occupied with remembering and belting out a singing role could possibly attend to the finer points of acting too. The broader points maybe, but not the finer ones.

Gestures

Fortunately very few opera libretti demand much in the way of finesse or depth. Opera singers, over the centuries, have therefore learned special methods of portraying these fundamental facets of human emotions.

A few expressions can be made by such elementary contortions as:
- forehead-furrowing
- eye-widening
- brow-raising.

Unfortunately, few of these subtle touches are really noticeable on the distant opera stage; and certainly not in Earls Court. So the basic points have to be made with the arms. There are three standard gestures used:
1) Arms or arm outspread express generalised joy and euphoria. This is usually only needed in the early scenes as most operas tend to get more lugubrious as the action proceeds.

) Arms or arm across the bosom or chest signifies sincerity. This is very useful throughout as a general antidote to the obvious insincerity of most libretti.

) One arm across the forehead, palm uppermost, indicates despair, remorse, confusion, hopelessness, pain – or all at once. This gesture is more frequently drawn into use as the opera proceeds; at which stage it can also indicate a forgotten line.

Few opera plots ask for more than this apart from an bility to handle a death scene. These most commonly nvolve considerable use of gesture (3) with one arm, vhile the other arm indicates the point where the ndividual has been stricken, e.g.

- stomach or throat for poisoning
- middle of the back for stabbing
- chest for TB.

Ie or she staggers about quite a bit, leaning on any table hat happens to be around, and knocking over a few hairs. The fall to the ground is most effective on a flight of tairs, and everyone assumes it is all over. Mainly for the ake of comfort, they then prop themselves up on one arm, r perhaps recline in the arms of the loved one, and sing nother last aria or two, generally on the subject of better ays.

Props

)pera singers must also be adept at wearing masks for he purpose of concealing their identity from spouse or amily while carrying on an adulterous under-plot, and nale singers are expected to be able to fight with swords nd things. The main concern here is, of course, not to get eriously hurt and the general lack of skill displayed can ause anxious moments for everybody both on and off tage.

Voices

The minimal acting requirements seen to, the singer can concentrate on singing. Most singers would prefer to be either sopranos or tenors as these voices nearly always get the longest and most virtuosic parts. Sopranos are notably temperamental. In the past they always used to be well-endowed and, indeed, plenty of busty substance was once considered an essential adjunct to a powerful and gallery-rattling voice. In more recent times there have been slender and attractive sopranos who are naturally in great demand and even more temperamental than their predecessors. Mezzo-sopranos generally have to be content with secondary parts, while contraltos often end up as nannies or elderly noblewomen. Baritones tend to be cuckold husbands while basses are nearly always villains.

You should be well acquainted with the categories of operatic voice for much is made in operatic tittle-tattle of their ranges and whether the possessors of them are capable of operating in the categories to which they claim to belong.

Male:

Castrati

These were fellows who had had things done to them at an early stage in their career which there is really no need to detail in conversation unless you happen to be talking to a musical medic.

Anyway, the voices that resulted soared to a stratospherically high range with a quality somewhat similar to the voice of an innocent choirboy; when there were such things. Although the sound achieved was of unsurpassed purity and clarity and of greater voluptuousness and strength than the average soprano's, and consequently in great demand, there was never a very big queue for the necessary operation, certainly not on a voluntary basis, and the occupation went out of fashion.

Those composers who still wanted to write for castrati were told to go and do it themselves so they quickly gave up the idea. Instead women were allowed to dress up as men (popularly known as breeches boys) to play youthful parts like Cherubino or Prince Orlofsky. The last castrati disappeared in the early 1900s, leaving no descendants. Once castrati had gone out of supply, if high-pitched men were wanted they had to make do with:

Countertenors

the ones who are noteworthy for their inability to sound anything like castrati. Their efforts always have a strained quality and are a source of embarrassment to many people. It is supposed to be done naturally and without any hint of falsetto, but seldom is. It was a popular range of voice up to the 18th century and was commercially revived in recent times by Alf Deller. These singing shop assistants (as they are laughingly known in the trade) have now become quite popular again; in fact there were so many of them around that a lot of them have had to go into pop groups and the King's Singers.

Tenors

have always been required to have strong and piercing voices capable of reaching from middle C to C'' and even beyond in bel canto operas like *Il Pirata* (who was known as the King of the High C's). Traditionally they have been small, stout men with big chests and dark hair who are expected to look romantic and handsome but more often look like ice-cream sellers or all-in wrestlers. The Italian variety go in for head notes which come out through their noses and they sob a good deal. They are categorised according to the parts they play as:

spinto (nasal)
grazia (that will do thank you)
buffo (well-oiled) or
forza (hard-pressed).

The German variety are of a more heroic nature and are known as *heldentenors* or *lyrischer* (wordy), *spiel* (garrulous), or *hoher* (verbose).

The very best tenors come from Sweden but the Swedes tend to be alcoholics. English tenors sing tones that many critics describe as white. More often they remind the listener of spa water without the sparkle. Americans are much the same except that they do it in American and consequently spoil the flavour of any role they undertake.

Baritones

are much the same as tenors except that they are taller and are only expected to go up to about G'. They are divided into similar categories and get some very good parts like Figaro and Papageno. Unfortunately they are often required to be comedians.

Basses

are often, for some obscure reason, smaller and thinner than tenors and baritones, though not always. They are not required to go up at all but are expected to go down to the point where the pitch ceases to be comprehensible. These are known as footnotes. Many of them are of slavonic origin and they get good parts in Russian operas, but otherwise play the parts of bad people like Sarastro and tend to get married off to the contraltos. Those who will sink to any depth are known as basso profundos which does not mean that they are profound in any way.

There are also comic basses, bass buffo, who have fun in parts like Osmin, Bartolo and Jetsam. Basses and baritones who are incapable, respectively, of going low or high enough are called bass-baritones.

Female:

Sopranos

are often better when surrounded by a good protective
layer and have been known to go off when they paid too
much attention to the current trends and tried to lose
weight. The thin, glamorous ones never seem to last
beyond a season or two. Sopranos are supposed to go up to
F''' or thereabouts. It is said that Mozart helped one
reluctant soprano to achieve this range by reaching out
from behind the curtain and pinching her bottom. But
most of them do try, some even too much, as the high
flyers get all the best operatic roles like Tosca, Queen of
the Night and Brünnhilde.

Mezzo-Sopranos (*Eng.* messy sopranos)

are those who got stuck a few notes short of where they
intended to go.

Contraltos or Altos

are female singers with deep voices who either sing
elderly parts or pretend to be men. There was once a well-
loved contralto called Kathleen Ferrier who sang the part
of Orfeo. But most of them, especially those with very deep
voices who sound as though they had beards, have to be
content with parts in *The Merry Wives of Windsor* or *HMS
Pinafore*, and are generally deprived of love scenes.

Top Notes (which have always been very much a
talking point in opera):

The first tenor high C'' is said to have been achieved by
one Duprez back in the 1830s. It was rather like running
the first 4-minute mile and seems to have taken an undue
amount of effort at the time in view of its frequent
attainment since. Rossini, who had a cruel tongue, said

that Duprez's high C sounded like 'the squawk of a capon whose throat was being cut'. On the whole composers much preferred their singers to hover decently around G. Sopranos, on the other hand, are expected to hit stratospheric notes with ease. The whole thing becomes a bit of a trial for everyone when the singer is quite obviously building up to some new clearance; particularly when she fails to make it. Worst of all is the soprano who has managed to achieve the sort of projection that ensures high and shrill top notes but has done herself permanent damage in the lower register and becomes inaudible in sub-stratospheric passages. Generally speaking the singers with the greatest agility and range tend to be the least intelligible. You can't have everything.

A Few Good Phrases

The bluffer should be acquainted with a few basic terms of criticism, one of the favourites being 'insecure above the stave'. To be considered insecure below it would, of course, be the ultimate condemnation.

'insecure above the stave' – wobbles on the high notes

'hardens above the stave' – the high notes sound as if someone has trodden on the cat's tail

'brilliantly sustained throughout its range' – sings just as loudly at any pitch

'a well-schooled voice' – dull

'innate musicianship' – not bad

'supreme exponent of bel canto' – goes in for lots of trills and things

'has become a legend' – dead for a long time

has become a legend in his/her lifetime' – passed his/her prime

technically perfect' – dull

excels in the more lyrical roles' – musical but unintelligent

avoidance of all exaggeration' – doesn't get excited

her singing compensates for any dramatic limitations' – can't act for toffee

a wide vibrato' – sustained wobble

the artistry is still there' – can no longer sing

lack of inner fire' – dull

flawless legato' – doesn't articulate

inclined to over sentimentalise' – a ham

breathing noisy' – inclined to snort

in later years the voice darkened' – could no longer reach the high notes

has become a little mannered' – full of irritating tricks

moves easily on the stage' – rarely falls over

wisely limits his/her appearances' – is really past it

Voices of the Past

A debate in which the operatic bluffer is bound to get caught up concerns the relative merits of past stars of the operatic stage and those of today.

The side to take is easily decided upon, being simply the opposite of what the other person is saying. If they say that the singers of yore were better, you maintain that we have never had it so good. Fortunately, whatever you believe, there is no way of proving it. The only tangible evidence, which isn't really tangible at all, is a number of old 78 rpm recordings, those that escaped being made into flower pots during one or other of the wars; and what comes out of those is mainly inclined to make you feel that nobody could sing in tune at all.

We are assured however by John Freestone and other venerable survivors that the piping noises that issue forth are golden voices of the past. There was, of course, nobody more revered than Enrico Caruso, the prototype plump tenor who could soar and sob with the best of them, hitting high Cs for six and wowing the critical audiences of La Scala where he was the originator of many famous roles. At first, so they say, it was all technical wizardry but later, after some nodular trouble, he had to go easy on the high notes and go for the heavier dramatic stuff like *I Pagliacci*. But was he greater than the supreme *bel cantoist* Mattia Battistini, 'La Gloria d'Italia', or Fernando de Lucia, *tenore de grazia* supreme, or the great Jean de Reszke; or the later Beniamino Gigli who was Caruso all over again, or Giovanni Martinelli whose hand we once shook?

Those who are not over keen on the Italian sob stuff and prefer to base their opinions on something a bit more hi-fi, may well rate Jussi Björling amongst the best, preferring to ignore the stories of his battle with the bottle. If you like a bit of eccentricity plump for John McCormack and Richard Tauber. The voices of today faction may well thrust Pavarotti, Domingo and Carreras upon you in CD sound but if they do, merely sharpen your thorn needle and harken back to dimmer days. The greatest bass of all time is held to be Feodor Chaliapin, but one has to admit that he was a bit of a ham. The finest baritone we heard was Tito Gobbi and we have his autograph. Then there is Dietrich Fischer-Dieskau for the thinking man.

Amongst the great women it is churlish to suggest anything less than sainthood for such redolent names as Jenny Lind – the Swedish nightingale, Adelina Patti – the Spanish snack, Amelia Galli-Curci – the Italian main dish, Emmy Destinn – the bouncing Czech, Rosa Ponselle – the American warbler, or Nellie Melba – the Australian dessert. On the other hand the unpredictable genius of 'la Diva' Maria Callas can be heard more clearly and you are on safe ground with Flagstad, Supervia, Schumann and Lehmann who are no longer with us. Everyone reveres Eva Turner, and for the others who are still around, some of them big and strong, Sutherland, Berganza, Schwarzkopf, Price, Turner, all is admiration. We simply love Kiri Te Kanawa's accent and we are infatuated by Frederica Von Stade. But this must remain a secret.

The thing to remember is that no-one today can do it like they used to.

OPERA PLOTS

The opera plot is generally referred to as the *libretto* from the Italian meaning 'little book' – i.e. 'small', 'insignificant' and 'hardly worth reading'. Few have actually read a libretto for its own sake or, if they have it must have been for a desperate lack of something else to do.

Although there appears to be a wide range of subject matter covered, in fact the kinds of operatic libretti available are very limited. The illogical nature of opera seems to have led to a thorough-going illogicality in all departments of the art. Whereas the straight theatre likes a semblance of reality to enliven what is going on, some reflection of actual life, the opera never gave a thought to such matters. What goes on in an opera, as Hazlitt said, is what was never said, thought or done anywhere else but in an opera.

Many classical opera plots demand that at least one central character shall be raving mad. All the other characters are mad to a lesser degree, and all behave in a totally irrational manner. Which is not really all that surprising when you consider that they are having to sing everything they feel.

Somewhere at the heart of all grand operas of the early Italian kind lies the same plot with tiny variations.

Plot of Opera:
There is some kind of nobleman around, ranging from a Emperor or King at the top level to some decaying Duke at the bottom. He is generally the one who is mad in a King Lear-like sort of way. Mind you, he is rightly mad, because his estate is in a sorry state of decline and everyone is trying to do him out of what remains, especially his wicked brother who is only there to provide a suitable bass role, but has seized on his chance of a bit of skulduggery.

The nobleman (let us call him the Duke of Lasagne) has a beautiful daughter who is in love with a handsome but penniless swineherd. Marriage to him is, of course, out of the question because the perilous financial state of Lasagne demands that she marries the son of the Duke of Taglioni who is excessively wealthy and only too ready to add Lasagne to his company interests. Depending on how long they want the opera to go on, this is the set up for various possible solutions.

In a number of operas it is soon evident that the swineherd is in fact the young heir to the Taglioni fortunes but he is much too dumb to say so and get it all over with. The daughter, on the other hand, deeply as she is in love with him, fails to recognise him because of the swine droppings with which he is covered. Either she eats out her heart for two acts before they come to the happy ending that could easily have been arrived at two acts ago; or, if the librettist and composer have dramatic pretensions, she will take poison, kindly offered to her by her ugly stepsister, and die at great length somewhere near the end of the opera in his, the disguised prince's arms. This is a shame, for by now he has cleaned himself up and put on a new pair of tights and looks quite respectable.

A very large percentage of opera plots depend upon somebody not knowing somebody else, even someone as close as a wife or husband, because he or she is thinly disguised by a tiny mask that would not fool anyone outside an opera for one moment. Others depend on the main character being blinded by jealousy. Operatic characters are unsurpassably jealous and fly into complicated time signatures at the drop of a hat. The story of *Otello* provides opera with one of its most typical plots as the hero believes the worst of everybody, including his wife whose opaque arias immediately convince everyone but him of her total incapacity for deception.

It is fairly safe to make up bits of an opera plot as nobody is likely to challenge its validity. A fair number of them are just as unintelligible after reading the synopsis as before. The whole point in having opera mainly in a foreign language is that the plot can be totally ignored. While trying to work out what was happening you could miss some very pleasant music, so it is best not to bother.

USEFUL OPERAS

While it is undeniably useful to have a minimal knowledge of the standard repertoire, the true bluffer needs to have plenty of obscure fodder on the tip of his tongue. It is advisable to know:
a)   some works that are well and truly out of fashion
b)   things that those with whom you may bandy are not likely to know too well
c)   (in the last resort) a few that others have never even heard of.
You must choose the degree of obscurity according to the occasion. If, for instance, you are talking to dedicated Wagnerites, they will probably be unacquainted with anything of a more popular nature. Try first those operas that used to be popular in Victorian times but have since fallen out of critical favour because of their general lack of obscurity and tone. They should, however, be ones that have at least been recorded and may even be on a CD, as this gives extra weight to your enthusiasm.

For example, you might indicate a great affection for *Martha* [pronounced Mar-tar] by Friedrich von Flotow [pronounced Flo-toe], whose tuneful unharmfulness has frequently urged critics to refer to it in such jocular terms as something 'to cheer a cold winter's evening' – which they would never expect or even like Wagner to do – and to have slyly dubbed its main characters as 'heartless

30

Harriet and luckless Lionel'.

Plot of Martha:

The nobly born Harriet, bored with high life, goes off with her companion Nancy to Richmond Fair, both disguised as servant girls (i.e. with slightly dirty faces, untidy hair and pinafores), calling themselves Martha and Julia (which are actually considered to be better-class names today, but that is by the way). There they are hired by two farmers, luckless Li and his friend who has the unlikely name of Plunkett. Rather than reveal their true noble identities, the girls quickly decide to go along with the general idea and thus find themselves in the roles of two incompetent kitchen maids. Holding the job long enough to fall in love, Martha with Li and Julia with Plunk, they eventually make their escape.

Some time later, in another act, Li and Plunk are having a noggin outside their local when a royal hunting party comes by amongst whom they recognise Harriet and Nancy, now in aristocratic garb. But when Li says 'hi', she has him arrested in order to keep up appearances in front of the Queen. Li, however, has a ring which he manages to get to her Majesty and which proves that he is none other than the missing Earl of Derby. Which is about as unlikely as anything you are likely to find in opera. He is still a bit put out at her treatment of him but relents, in true operatic fashion, when she sings 'The last rose of summer' (which Fred Flo-toe pinched from Tom Moore's collection of Irish melodies) and they are soon happily reunited. Luckless Earl Li also has a good hit number called 'Ach, so fromm' (*Italian*: 'M'appari'; *English*: 'She appeared like a star') which the Victorians were very fond of.

One can understand the revulsion that any well-bred opera-lover might feel toward such a soppy opus and a ruthless enough bluffer could do well to push it hard.

Other (recorded) operas that come into this sort of category are:

a) *Tiefland* by Eugen d'Albert (whose father was a dance band leader), a work full of good tunes and left-wing leanings;

b) *La Muette de Portici* or *Masaniello* by Daniel Auber [pronounced oh-bear];

c) *The Bohemian Girl* by Michael Balfe (whose father taught dancing and who was himself a fiddler and a popular singer), a work full of such Victorian drawing-room material as 'I dreamt I dwelt in marble halls' (a chilling experience one would have thought) and 'When other lips'. It made him a fortune in 1843 and second-hand copies of the score can be found almost anywhere. Carrying a well-worn copy at an operatic party could do wonders.

Next, consider operas whose existence clearly cannot be denied since somebody has somehow found the cash to record them, but which history has generally overlooked. Usually, when you hear them, you can understand why, but this need not be a deterrent to your social championship of them. Some suggested titles that have recently appeared are:

a) *Sigurd* by Ernest Reyer which unfortunately chose a story that Wagner had already flogged for all it was worth and which Saint-Saëns described as being 'put together like a penny dreadful';

b) *Guercoeur* by Albéric Magnard which is as heavy going as anything you are likely to come across.

Alternatively, you could go for something modern and inexplicable like *The Knot Garden* or something by Stockhausen, but it is easy to get caught out in these areas if you meet somebody who reads *Opera* or knows Oliver Knussen.

Finally there is an endless supply of operas which nobody has heard of at all, except mad lexicographers. But there is really not a lot of point in citing something that nobody knows of as they might simply believe that you have made it up. It is, clearly, much better to make up titles and have them thought real, than to use real titles and have them disbelieved.

You can't go wrong, in Italian vein, with a few phoney kings like *Arthriticus, Re de Venuzzio*, or such noblemen as *Il Conte de Monte Vani*; or even commoners like *Maria de Milton Keynes* (based on the Scott novel). And who is to know that there is no such composer as 'Verimini' or 'Tomihandli'. Don't overdo this as you could make up a name like *Le Brasseur de Preston* only to find it is genuine.

Best of all, as always in better-class bluffing, is to have some genuine rarities up your sleeve and express great surprise that your opponent is not intimately acquainted with Liszt's *Don Sanche*; Sibelius's *Jungfrun i tornet*; or Kuhlau's [pronounced Koo-low] *Lulu*; all of which are surprisingly good. Actually one bluffer we know got thrown out of a party for asking a lady if she had "ever seen Kuhlau's *Lulu?*". She was just about to say 'No, but she had seen Berg's'.

OPERETTA

This is a special kind of lightweight opera for those who cannot take the real thing. Rather like a curry without any curry powder in it. The stories are just as confusing and involved as in opera but are more directly conveyed in large slabs of unrealistic dialogue. In between there are disconnected songs that are either of a lightly romantic or coyly comic nature. There are no death scenes, mad scenes or stabbings in operetta and everything ends happily with the hero marrying the heroine, the hero's friend marrying the heroine's friend and the funny man marrying the funny lady. There is quite an obsession with the desirability of getting married.

Operetta came into fashion round about 1850 in response to the new spending power of the middle classes who never liked art to be too arty and were fond of a good tune. It was invented in Paris by a German Jew called Offenbach, much to the indignation of the opera authorities there who refused to allow such lowbrow goings-on in their theatres. To get round this Offenbach started his own theatre, a very small and uncomfortable place where he staged naughty little shows in which the characters danced around in short skirts and made fun of the establishment. These had genuinely witty tunes – a thing unheard of in opera – and they soon caught on in places like London and Vienna.

In London the idea was taken up by Gilbert & Sullivan who gave it a comfortably Victorian feel; and in Vienna by people like Suppé and Johann Strauss who found that all they had to do was put some dialogue in between their waltzes and the thing was almost ready-made.

The idea was also exploited by a lot of Hungarian bandmasters like Franz Lehár and sung by romantic tenors with monocles. It soon caught on in America as well where it was written by even more Hungarian bandmasters who had fled from some revolution or other, and an occasional Irishman.

Without noticeably altering the pattern of things, operetta became even less operatic as audiences of even lower brows acquired a taste for singing. Calling itself musical comedy, it was now made up of slabs of unrealistic dialogue interspersed with disconnected songs of a lightly romantic or coyly humorous nature, and had stories in which the hero married the heroine, the hero's friend married the heroine's friend and the funny man married the funny lady. The only real difference was that it was all jazzed up a bit. Later things went full circle and musical comedy began to take itself seriously. This was achieved by dropping the comedy bit and simply calling itself The Musical.

The final advancement was that some operettas returned to being indistinguishable from opera and were written by clever men with names like Sondheim. Others moved into the pop field and disguised any lack of real distinction by being deafeningly amplified.

MODERN STUFF

Opera houses, because of their subsidies, feel compelled to put on modern things occasionally but their audiences noticeably fall off when they do, and most of the time it's back to Verdi, Puccini and *Cav* and *Pag*.

All significant modern opera falls into three types:

1. Operas with no tunes and little action
2. Operas with action but few tunes
3. Schoenberg.

The stories are expositions of psychiatric case histories and very few end in marriage or any other kind of perpetuation of the species. However modern opera caters for a very élite audience with a high degree of mental endurance, so you are fairly safe at all times. Have some plot or other to hand, let us say *Lulu* for instance, and move the conversation toward it at crucial moments.

Plot of Lulu:

Lulu, dressed as a pierrot, is having her portrait painted while Dr.Schön looks on. Dr.Schön goes off with his son and Lulu seduces the painter. Lulu's husband enters and dies of a heart attack when he sees them at it. Lulu marries the painter, but now seduces Dr.Schön. Who is this doctor anyway and why hasn't he been struck off the register? The painter comes in and finds them at it and shoots himself. Lulu now works on Schön, whom she has known since she was a toddler and who is infatuated with her although temporarily engaged to someone else. They get married but Lulu now seduces Alwa, Schön's neurotic son; you remember him from way back. Lulu also has an affair with a lesbian Countess and a couple of ambiguous lads from the chorus. Schön is jealous and tries to get Lulu to shoot herself but she is strongly against this idea and shoots him instead. Lulu escapes from prison, with the Countess taking her place, and seduces Alwa again. In the last scene Lulu is embroiled with a Count Casti Piani in Paris. He is a nasty bit of work. She escapes from him and becomes a prostitute in London. She is followed there by neurotic Alwa and the lesbian Countess; Alwa is killed by one of her clients. Finally both Lulu and the Countess are killed by none other than Jack the Ripper, who was looking around for a role in a musical at the time.

Anyone who can remember all that clearly has nothing better to occupy their mind.

COMPOSERS

In the opera world, in spite of strong action taken by successive generations of singers, opera composers have managed to hold their own. In fact, opera lovers are frequently able to distinguish between the operas of, let us say, Donizetti and Bellini, and know immediately whose it is. So they claim.

Opera composers tend to write operas and not much else and it is these we mainly deal with below. Only one composer, he who was the greatest of them all, can be said to have had an equal footing in the operatic and non-operatic worlds and that, of course, was

Mozart (1756-1791)
who found time, in between writing well over 600 highly esteemed Koechels (as his works are uniquely known), to pen such operatic masterpieces as K384, K492, K527, K588 and K620, not to mention K366, K621 (which have recently come back into favour) and lesser items like K50, K51, K135, K196, K208, K486 and many other scattered fragments. The astute bluffer could achieve a remarkably quick victory by asking people what they think of K87 or K111.

Mozart can be said to have put opera into modern shape, particularly with K492 which told an everyday story of servant folk, mixed in with a few nobles, of course, (but then you can't do everything at once) and was packed full of good tunes which the composer was delighted to find errand boys whistling in the street and being purveyed by barrel organs. He knocked it out in a few weeks in a dark little room in Vienna near the cathedral and his favourite pubs and snack bars and *The Marriage of Figaro* turned out to be one of the most perfect operas ever written.

Who does not know and love items No.9 (so splendidly used as a military march) and the graceful No.10 from

K492; the immortal invitation to give me thy hand
(unfrozen variety) from K527 (*Don Giovanni*); the wholly
delectable score of K588 an immaculate little farce about
marital love under test conditions (sometimes known
under its undecipherable code name of *Così fan tutte*,
which roughly translates as 'women are like that'); or
songs sung by such unforgettable characters as the
birdcatcher and the Queen of the Night in K620 (*The
Magic Flute*), which all agree is an absolute rag-bag of
shapeless nonsense, but a splendid opera.

There is plenty of scope for lesser-known Mozart titles
that one may toss around – e.g. *Mitridate, Ascanio in
Alba, Il Sogno di Scipione, Zaide* and *La finta semplice*;
not to mention such unfinished morsels as *L'Oca del Cairo*
and *Lo Sposa deluso*.

After Mozart, the big two specialists of opera are Verdi
and Wagner.

Verdi (1813-1901)
Son of a village innkeeper, Verdi was one of the world's
legion of small men who make such an indelible mark on
its history and achievements. All his adult life he looked
like a professional anarchist, with a pale pock-marked
countenance which he hid behind a conspiratorial sort of
beard, the sinister effect given the final touch by his
addiction to dark, wide-brimmed hats. His character was
in keeping with this appearance – silent, moody, pugna-
cious and tough.

The resolve that later carried him through such a vast
acreage of work, enabled him to survive several initial
setbacks. First he was rejected by the Milan Conservatory
of Music and had to learn his art by listening to as much
music as he could and copying out the scores he most
admired. Next he failed to obtain a much desired
appointment as an organist. Then he had but a moderate

success with his first opera *Oberto* and was commissioned to write *Un Giorno di Regno* when both his children died and then his wife. Finally the opera was a complete failure. At this point he formed his public philosophy: 'I accept their criticism and jeers only on condition that I do not have to be grateful for their applause', grew his beard a bit more and had another try.

Accepting a libretto that had been turned down by Nicolai, he wrote *Nabucco*, a work of such sweeping fervour that the public could hardly help but notice it. Even the backstage people were so enraptured by the production they forgot to get on with their backstaging and listened to the opera instead. Particularly a chorus of Hebrew slaves, 'Va pensiero', which struck a special chord with the Italian public who were simmering under the yoke of the Austrians. It became a sort of subversive national anthem. In later years, it became a standby item with Welsh choirs and the slow march of the Grenadier Guards, but, sadly, Verdi was not able to appreciate these ultimate accolades. It did, however, make him the patron saint of the organ-grinders (a position later affirmed many times by such obvious barrel-organ material as 'La donna e mobile' – a song about women drivers). After that there was no stopping him and he wrote in similar vein in *I Lombardi* and *Ernani*.

When he came to *Macbeth* he was sufficiently emboldened to ask the singers to stop making beautiful but shallow noises and to sing the parts of villains as if they really meant it. He also suggested they confined themselves to the notes he had written, a hitherto unconsidered point of view that took a bit of getting used to. Wagner was having similar thoughts in Germany.

While he continued to provide traditional fare concerning erotic aristocrats and sheep-like peasants on an umpah-pah basis, his works were getting far more assertive. Between 1851-3 he produced *Rigoletto*, *Il Trovatore* and

La Traviata, with leadings parts for a hunchback, a consumptive and a gypsy respectively, parts which the singers quite enjoyed trying out even though the music had very little affinity with the subjects. It was at this time that the few stock gestures that pass for acting on the operatic stage were invented. Verdi also kindly provided singers with prolonged death scenes lasting up to half an hour, which allowed them to exhibit their vocal prowess right until the final moment when the stabbing or poisoning took effect and they fell with a dull thud upon the stage.

By now he could write more or less what he wanted. Coping with the customary supply of unsuitable libretti, he wrote rich scores in which the arias became increasingly a part of the drama rather than a showpiece for those endowed with good top notes. He also took up farming, travelled abroad and spent five years as a Member of Parliament.

In 1869 he was asked to write an opera for the opening of the Suez Canal. Failing to finish it he fobbed them off with another production of *Rigoletto*. The intended *Aida* was finally seen in Cairo in 1871 and Verdi didn't even bother to go and see his mammoth effort with parts for elephants and very large sopranos. (As she has to die in Radames' arms, he has to be big as well.) It's considered bad form to count how many times you can spot the chorus racing round the back of the pyramids to change hats and march staunchly across again during the interminable Triumphal March.

Hearing what Wagner was up to in Bayreuth, he decided that sterner stuff was needed and turned once more to Shakespeare, coping with the jealousies of Othello as successfully as he did with the philanderings of Falstaff. By now he was passing 80 and considered that he had long ago made up for his lack of inches and academic prowess. He had worn out many hats and had the pleasure

40

of hearing his tunes whistled by countless errand boys*. No more operas seemed to be needed to make the point. After founding a home for aged musicians in Milan which still lives off his royalties, he waited until the new century came in with all its attendant horrors and then died, as truculent as ever, in the Grand Hotel.

It is difficult to find rare Verdi pieces to have up your sleeve because there has been a determined effort to record the lot. But you might still get away with a declared preference for things like *Un giorno di regno* (which is good fun), *I Lombardi* (which also has a good Welsh-type chorus), *Alzira* and *Attila* (we forget which is which).

Wagner (1813-1883)

By an interesting quirk of fate, the world's greatest composer of Italian operas and the world's greatest composer of German operas – Richard 'The Ring' Wagner – were born in the same year, 1813. They were, however, totally different characters born in different months, so astrologer bluffers have no cause to get excited. And, whereas Verdi was slightly mad, Wagner was totally so.

He started off quietly enough in a sort of Beethovenish vein and his third opera *Rienzi*, for example, might easily have been written by Weber, if he hadn't been dead. Even the *Flying Dutchman* which followed had bits in it that

*Errand boys were at one time considered the final arbiters of a good tune – a highly useful service as critical opinion has always been far from unanimous on this particular subject. It was always considered a good selling point if a work could be said to be full of the sort of thing that 'could be whistled by errand boys'. Unfortunately, today not only are errand boys more a less an extinct species, but the few that can be found in remote country districts have lost the art of whistling and are more likely to be found listening to a portable form of radio. There are still paper boys but they tend to operate at very early hours so that they are discouraged from whistling and, on the whole, their contribution to musical taste has been negligible.

41

might have been written by Gilbert & Sullivan had they bucked up their ideas a bit. People might have known from *Tannhäuser* and *Lohengrin*, even though they contained excellent material for brass and military band use, just what was coming.

Early in his career he fled to London to avoid the debt collector along with a girl called Minna and a dog called Robber who caused them a lot of trouble with the authorities. They survived fog and storms and ended up in a pub in Old Compton Street, but during their stay all the people that Wagner wanted to see kept pretending to be out. They resumed a penniless existence in Paris and Wagner became a revolutionary character and took in lodgers. All these things clearly had a later effect on the course of his work. How else can one explain *The Ring*.

Saved by the 500 francs he got for *The Flying Dutchman* and the success of *Rienzi*, he went off to Dresden where he caused everybody a lot of trouble. Nevertheless he was showing them that opera was no laughing matter. He continued his revolutionary activities and was, of necessity, constantly on the move, still lugging Minna around and, by now, another dog called Peps and a parrot called Papo. His feeling for animals was about the only thing he shared with Verdi. Minna died in 1866 and he married Cosima, who had been the wife of his best friend, and they had two children. He also had a long-standing affair with Mathilde Wesendonck. Now he was on the verge of producing those great German operas, music by Wagner to words by Wagner, directed by Wagner, that had been in the back of his mind even in the old days in Compton Street. He sold the parrot and put the money toward building a personal opera house at Bayreuth. He was increasingly well in with the Emperor who came and stayed for a week in 1876 to hear *The Ring* performed. Success had not been gained without its penalties. Suffering from pains in the abdomen, heart trouble, rheumatism and something picked up from the parrot, his last years were spent in a state of suffering and depression, only made bearable by the conviction that he was God. By now Stravinsky had been born and Wagner gave up the ghost in 1883.

Wagner's *Ring* is the ultimate test of the dedicated opera lover. He took well over twelve years to write it and it can seem to take roughly the same time to perform if one is not a dedicated Wagnerian and able to take its complex mythology to heart. Those preparing themselves for the final assault can conveniently limber up on such modestly mountainous works as *Der fliegende Holländer* (it's not so long as his later pieces, reaching port after 2½ hours with a following wind); *Tannhäuser, Lohengrin, Tristan und Isolde* (which upsets some people because of its shamelessly erotic goings-on), *Die Meistersinger von Nürnberg* (which upsets nobody because there are no deaths and Wagner said it was a comedy), and *Parsifal*. Opera devotees are divided into two main groups, the Wagnerites and the others.

The Inis and the Ettis:

Puccini (1858-1924)

Puccini cleverly managed to combine being one of the most popular of all opera composers with looking like a rich gambler. Perhaps he was proving that they were the same thing. In his early days it took him quite a while to shake off the influence of his teacher Ponchielli – The Dance of the Hours and all that. Thus his first opera *Le Villi* told of a young man who goes off to seek his fortune so that he can marry his loved one. Unfortunately he gets in with a bad lot and forgets her and she dies of a broken heart. Eventually he remembers the original plan but when he returns he meets up with her ghost while some of

her witch friends dance round him till he drops dead a
well. As you may gather, it is not a cheerful piece and it
effect on audiences was such as to inaugurate the phras
'to have the willies'. Written originally for a competition
which was won by *Cavalleria Rusticana*, it ought to hav
taught him something. Instead, he wrote *Edgar*, the stor
of a tenor who falls equally for a soprano and a mezzo
soprano. Finally deciding on the soprano as the bette
operatic prospect he is stabbed in the middle-range by th
mezzo. As might be expected, this was a total failure.

Pulling himself together he chose something a bit mor
verismatic and utilised the best-selling *Manon Lescaut*. I
went down so well that, at the end, he had to take fift
curtain calls. He went on to such top hits as *La Bohème
Tosca*, *Madama Butterfly*, *La Fanciulla del West* an
Turandot. This he achieved with a melodic line whic
upset a lot of the contemporary critics by being s
blatantly sensational. It was simply that Puccini was wel
ahead of his time and anticipated the modern middle
class taste for treacly tunes and sugary harmonies and th
art of Mantovani and Lawrence Welk. *La Bohème* i
possibly the most popular opera of all time. Unfortunatel
it needs too many good singers which makes it a costl
affair at the going rate. Tautly written, expansivel
tuneful, expensively produced, it has everything going fo
it. *Tosca* is one of the most verismo of Puccini's operas
melodramatic and vulgarly musical with a jolly goo
villain called Scarpia and ending with Tosca jumping of
the local battlements, a device that can only be achieve
with the aid of something inflatable, and has on at leas
one occasion resulted in Tosca being bounced back.

It is difficult for the bluffer to find obscure Puccin
operas to trot out apart from those first-mentioned above
except for *La Rondine*, where he appears to have set out t
write a Viennese operetta but changed his mind halfwa
through Act 2 and World War I. Possibly the worst thing

he wrote was the hit song 'O my beloved daddy' which he threw in for good measure and no good reason in the middle of a bedroom farce called *Gianni Schicchi*. You could profess a great liking for it if you don't mind being thought rather lowbrow.

Donizetti (1797-1848)
Donizetti's parents didn't think that writing music was a good thing so he joined the Army. After he had been caught writing half-a-dozen or so operas in his off-duty moments he eventually got his discharge and settled down to a busy life composing a total of 75 and lots of other things as well like choral works and wind quintets.

A placid sort of fellow he worked at top speed (he considered Rossini a bit of a sluggard for taking two weeks to write an opera). All his operas are pleasantly alike and full of leaps and trills for the delight of prima donnas, his most likeable stuff being comedies such as *Don Pasquale* and *La Fille du Régiment* which gave people like Offenbach the idea for starting the operetta craze.

Donizetti's *L'Elisir d'Amore* was so quickly successful that it convinced a lot of writers thereafter, including W.S.Gilbert, that operas about elixirs were good box office. Unfortunately they didn't have a big hit like 'Una furtiva lagrima' for the glorification of tenors like Caruso, Gigli, Schipa, Pavarotti or Hubert Hardcastle (from our local operatic society). Furtive lagrimas were in even if elixirs never made it.

There is plenty of scope for bluffing in the Donizetti field as most of his operas are still unknown territory. Take your pick from such things as the early *Enrico di Borgogna*, the lugubrious *Don Sebastiano* which someone once described as 'a funeral in five acts', or the posthumous *Gabriella di Vergy*. You will hardly notice the difference. He was fond of operas about ladies from unlikely places such as Emily who came from Liverpool

and Lizzie from Kenilworth, and Lucy from Lammer
moor. A discussion of Donizetti's influence on the Mersey
side scene could perhaps prove quite fruitful.

Bellini (1801-1835)

came from Sicily and was encouraged to write hi
benevolently tuneful operas by a rich nobleman who pai
for his education. His first big success was *Il Pirata* whic
was liked because it was not as fussy as the operas o
Rossini who was then cornering the market in fiorituras

As any strong coffee addict will know, Bellini's *L
Somnambula* concerns a lady who sleepwalks. Its popu
larity with opera-goers arises from the famous scen
where the inevitably large prima donna needed for thi
sort of bel canto role walks across a bridge, long declare
unsafe by the local council, in her sleep and a frill
nightie. The bridge is supposed to collapse just after sh
has crossed it, but naturally there are always those in th
audience who hope that it might happen a bit earlie
There have been one or two disasters at this point; bu
most of them musical in origin. *Norma* concerns a highl
strung Druid priestess who has a penchant for burnin,
and otherwise killing people, with a lot of arias to ge
through to explain away her proclivities. In the end sh
repents and commits hari kari.

Bellini was the father of the drawing-room ballad
providing swooping melodies to banal words over a simpl
accompaniment. He was greatly admired by Chopin. H
unromantically died of dysentery at the age of 34, hi
constitution weakened by writing too many notes abov
the stave.

Rossini (1792-1868)

was a man after many people's hearts who disliked worl
and much preferred a life of eating, drinking and makin;
snide remarks about other composers. He built up ;

library of ready-made accompaniments, easy-to-fit decorative passages, infinitely-expandable terminal crescendos and interchangeable overtures (which have caused much needed employment for operatic researchers ever since).

He would send along bits of the score to the opera house while they were rehearsing the song before and, at the very last possible moment, he would deliver an already used overture with the old title scratched out. After being used for so many operas, the Overtures naturally became very well known and were much loved because of their crescendos. For every person who knows and buys a recording of a Rossini overture only approximately one-fiftieth of a person has actually heard the opera it came from – with the obvious exception of *The Barber* whose overture had already been used for two other operas. So a proclaimed acquaintance with *La Scala di Seta* or *La Gazza Ladra* may be good enough bluffing.

There are plenty of unknown Rossini operas which, shorn of their overture, provide good name-tossing material, e.g. all those double acts like *Demetrio e Polibo*, *Ricciardo e Zoraide*, *Edoardo e Cristina* or *Bianca e Faliero* which anybody could easily mix up. Then there is his Folies revue called *Il Viaggio a Reims* and five operas for L'Opéra, three of which were patched together, including *William Tell* which lasts for six hours and is actually two operas that had got stapled together by mistake but he didn't like to say so.

Rossini also created a few religious works, and a number of trifles he called *The Sins of Old Age* which were later bought as a job lot by Benjamin Britten. A good example of a snide Rossini remark is his declaration that Wagner's music had divine moments – but it was the hours that got him down. His joke book was later purchased by Sir Thomas Beecham.

Beethoven (1770-1827)

was not really an opera composer but he didn't like t
admit it. He only managed *Fidelio* which took him abou
nine years to get right and he did much better out o
writing nine symphonies. He did think of trying agair
with such subjects as Faust, Macbeth and Alexander the
Great in mind but each time he wisely decided to compose
another string quartet instead.

Bizet (1838-1875)

had rather a disappointing career as an opera composer
though one or two things like *Les Pêcheurs de Perles* and
La Jolie Fille de Perth were reasonably successful
Several, with rather awkward names like *Djamileh*
Malbrough s'en va-t-en guerre and *Sol-si-ré-pif-par*
(which was set in a Chinese fish and chip shop) were
comparative failures. Even *Carmen* which was to become
the most profitable hit opera of all time got off to a sticky
start. The critic of the *Boston Gazette* immortalised
himself by writing 'the air of the Toreador is the only bit o
"tune" in the opera, and this scarcely rises above the
vulgarity of Offenbach'. It remains the only opera ir
which the female chorus work in a cigarette factory. Bize
died soon after at the early age of 36 convinced that the
whole thing had gone up in smoke.

Boito (1842-1918)

was a prominent figure in the operatic and literary worlc
of his day and wrote two splendid librettos for Verdi -
Otello and *Falstaff* – which were universally admired. He
also wrote *La Gioconda* for Ponchielli but after he hac
heard The Dance of the Hours and 'Cielo e mar' he
changed his name to Tobia Gorrio, though many of the
critics saw through this thin disguise.

48

Borodin (1833-1887)
only actually completed one opera, patching the rest up,
Rossini-style, from bits of others. His best known work,
Prince Igor, was so long that, even though he worked on it
for twenty years, he didn't have time to finish it. His old
friends Glazunov and Rimsky-Korsakov carried on after
his death and made it even longer so that a number of
other people with names ending in ov have had to work
hard on it ever since. Most people remember it as the
opera in which a lot of Polovtsians keep dancing and for its
main aria 'Stranger in Paradise'.

Britten (1913-1976)
is the best known British composer abroad, perhaps
accounted for by the coincidence of his name.
   He devised a simple method of writing operas, giving
each of them a central character who looked, sang and
generally behaved like his good friend Peter Pears, then
changed the name of the character to something more
earthy like Peter Grimes, Albert Herring or Billy Budd.
Perhaps the system did tend to make them all sound the
same but it never seems to lessen their renown.

Cimarosa (1749-1801)
worked in Russia for a time for Catherine the Great but
got dismissed for behaving in an Italian manner. On his
way home he passed through Vienna where he composed
an opera for the Emperor called *Il matrimonio segreto*
which the Emperor liked so much that he gave it the
unique distinction of being the only opera to be repeated
the same evening. It was quite short and he probably had
nothing else to do that night.

Debussy (1862-1918)
may have been a one-opera man, but it is one that people
have talked about ever since. *Pelléas et Mélisande* is

probably one of the most static operas ever written; with virtually no tunes in it and hardly any action. People mainly sit around and make ethereal noises. But there is one interesting moment when Mélisande, who has very long symbolic hair, lets it down over a balcony and Pelléas climbs up it.

Giordano (1867-1948)
set out to be an opera composer and turned out quite a lot. But being called Umberto seemed to tell against him and he only managed one best seller in *Andrea Chénier*, a sorry tale in which the hero and heroine end up under the guillotine. The only way he could see to a happy ending was marrying a rich lady; which he did and lived happily ever after.

Gluck (1714-1787)
Christoph Willibald Gluck, Willi to his friends, went to London in 1745 and met Handel. It was hearing Handel's operas that decided him against the conventional forms of Italian opera and he started out to change things a bit: firstly by making the whole thing more dramatic, and secondly by asking the singers to stop messing about. A modest man and a nice chap, with a crush on Iphigenia, he occasionally got their co-operation and had a big success with *Orfeo e Euridice*, starring Kathleen Ferrier. Unfortunately he met up with Salieri in Paris and died a few days later.

Gounod (1818-1893)
was as comfortably Victorian a composer as you can get and enjoyed great acclaim in his day. The cruel critics have since pointed out that he was totally inadequate in things like *Faust*, at one time one of the most popular operas ever written, which he packed full of rollicking choruses of peasants and soldiers, swinging waltzes and

sentimental songs about jewels and people who were quaintly chaste and demure, when he ought to have been producing something grim and intense. (The modern age is so ashamed of *Faust* that it has only had a handful of recordings in thirty years as compared with *La Forza del Destino* which gets at least one a year. *Faust* now ranks with Grieg's *Peer Gynt* as one of the great artistic misconceptions of all time.)

Gounod was equally lacking in profundity whether dealing with Goethe or Shakespeare and is clearly due for a big revival when the pendulum swings. Good long odds bet for any bluffer.

Handel (1685-1759)

muffled potential criticism with sheer weight of output. The reviews were hardly out before the next opera came along and people probably got confused as to which one they were listening to, particularly as they nearly always had brief proper names as their title. 'Do you remember that bit in *Alessandro* that went um-tiddle-tum?' 'No, that was in *Admeto*, surely!' 'We went to see *Ezio* last week – or was it *Sosarme*?' 'It must have been *Sosarme. Ezio* was on a month ago'. 'What do you think of *Orlando*?' 'That's next month.' 'Of course, how silly of me.'

Handel, being an amiable man and a bit deaf, was happy to turn out basic material, the only change being increased economy of means as he got older and wiser. He was actually a bit of a nuisance. Having spent his early days in Germany before a five-year stay in Italy where he picked up all the operatic dodges, he came to England and settled in London. He was the main reason why so little English opera ever got written. Which may, of course, have been a good thing. In the end, even he got fed up with opera singers and turned to oratorio with equal industry, achieving his No.1 hit with *Messiah*.

Humperdinck (1854-1921)

according to the historians, was a dedicated apostle of
Wagner. Which may explain why most of his operas are
seldom heard. Deserting the cause briefly and rediscover-
ing the delights of Weber, he wrote *Hänsel und Gretel*
whose top tune was taken up by children's choirs
everywhere with universal success.

Janáček (1854-1928)

was only known outside Czechoslovakia for many years
by his early opera *Její Pastorkyna*, which displayed his
background of Moravian folksong and the turgid family
life of the average Slav, but has latterly been discovered
and found to be ideal for stereophonic sound. So that, with
much help from his agent, Charlie Mackerras, *Príhody
Lisky Bystrousky*, *Vec Makropulos*, *Z mrtvého Domu* and
others have become commercially viable, as they say at
Covent Garden. We hope that serious bluffers will be
prepared to acquire a passable Czechoslovakian accent.
They can be bought quite cheaply from almost any
printer.

Leoncavallo (1858-1919) & Mascagni (1863-1945)

The Simon & Garfunkel of their day who wrote an opera
called *Cav e Pag*, which became vastly popular and is still
frequently played and recorded. Falling out over who had
written what and which, they embarked on solo careers
and were seldom heard of again.

Massenet (1842-1912)

was a typically French composer who wrote unmistakably French music to unmistakably French words. His
music has the consistency of a good bouillabaisse and his
stories are full of dark passion. Fashionable in his time
and having a fair success with *Manon*, recent recorded
revivals of his repertoire are easily available from the

remainder shelves. A casual knowledge of how his operas end could be good bluffing material.

Menotti (b. 1911)
stirred the opera world of the 1940s and 50s by writing some modern operas (*The Medium, The Telephone, Amahl and the Night Visitors, The Consul*) that had a popular vogue and upset the critics. He combines a Puccini-like sentimentality with stories utilising real people. Now out of fashion and not a good line to pursue, but due for a comeback.

Meyerbeer (1791-1864)
His real name, which he went to great lengths to conceal, was Jakob Liebmann Beer which would have been all right had his career been in the brewery business, but not much good for opera. He wrote the grandest of grand operas which, like Gounod's, are let down by corny little tunes that got into the Star Folios and are of the despised well-loved category. His critical esteem never recovered and he is now only revived as an example to young composers of what not to do if you want to get your operas put on in places other than Cardiff.

Monteverdi (1567-1643)
The Andrew Lloyd Webber of his day, Monteverdi often had several shows running at the same time. A lot of it, then considered expendable, but that would now fetch quite a good price, got lost, but most people would agree that there is quite enough left and a little of it goes quite a long way.

Compared to Peri's, Caccini's and Cavalli's, his works may seem to be teeming with life and intensely dramatic, but to modern ears they are fairly static. People stand around for a good deal singing away at one another, progress greatly hampered by the fact that all Monteverdi's characters have stutters* and thus take a long time getting their words out.

His most popular piece, *L'Incoronazione di Poppea*, was written when he was 75 and he therefore didn't get much of a reward for it. Many people will have vivid memories of the Glyndebourne production of *Il Ritorno d'Ulisse in Patria* in which gods and angels and other heavenly artisans kept descending from the flies on decorative window-cleaning platforms. First the feet, and then some legs, hairy or otherwise, would appear and the audience were kept happy making bets as to whom they belonged.

Nicolai (1810-1849)
wrote an opera whose overture was so enjoyable that people tended to put it on again and forget to listen to the rest of the opera. This is a pity because it is one of those rare cases where an opera is almost as good as its overture. It should be referred to as *Die lustigen Weiber von Windsor* [pronounced 'Vindsaw']. It also ends happily.

Offenbach (1819-1880)
Les Contes d'Hoffmann was the attempt of an established jester to do a musical Hamlet, to prove his serious capabilities. He needn't really have worried for the effort helped kill him and he never lived to see it staged. It turned out not half as memorable as his best funnies except where it was written in his lighter style. It gives good value to any soprano who is allowed, as Offenbach intended, to play all four roles of Olympia, Giuletta, Antonia and Stella, though they don't generally get paid four times as much.

*technically known as a bleat; *Ger:* Bockstrille.

Paisiello (1740-1816)
wrote over 100 operas and was doing very well until Rossini came along. His *Il Barbiere di Siviglia* was a great favourite and Rossini didn't please the Paisiello fan clubs of Bologna, Moderna, Parma and Naples by pinching the plot and writing a superior work. Rossini had taken the precaution of asking Paisiello if he minded and, of course, Paisiello had to say he didn't; and anyway, he didn't really expect Rossini's version to be better. There may be some mileage here in coming down in favour of Paisiello.

Ponchielli (1834-1886)
wrote an opera that had a popular ballet, called 'The Dance of the Hours' in the middle of it. This was so liked (and publicised by Walt Disney) that nobody really wanted to hear the rest of *La Gioconda*. Actually, they didn't miss much.

Smetana (1824-1884)
known to his family as Bedrich, was full of nationalist fervour and wrote some very tedious operas. However, he redeemed himself by achieving one jolly folk number, *Prodaná nevesta* (The battered bride) which is particularly well-known in orchestral excerpts. His career had an unbalancing effect on Smetana who went deaf and, later, mad.

Strauss (1864-1949)
was no relation of Johann and the rest, a disappointment which spurred him into writing *Der Rosenkavalier* and spitefully out-waltzing even the Strausses. He wrote other pleasantly demanding works in this vein, but revealed a split personality by writing purposefully nasty works like *Salome* and *Elektra*. He was one of the cleverest orchestrators of all time and has come in for a lot of criticism.

One of the fraternity described his music as 'aesthetically criminal and ill-mannered' and another suggested that he was better at orchestrating a bank account than music. He generally induces critics to go too far.

Thomas [pronounced Tom-are] (1811-1896)

was guilty of writing a gavotte and other tuneful pieces which he included in an opera called *Mignon*. Obviously not a man to be taken seriously.

Thomson (1896-1989)

wrote with an admirable economy of means; generally one note per syllable. As he chose Gertrude Stein as his librettist and nobody could understand what she meant, Thomson was widely praised for his sensitive setting of the American language. He wrote *Four Saints in Three Acts* (or was it *Three Saints in Four Acts* – one gets confused) and *The Mother Of Us All*. He also enjoyed being a critic and was mostly unkind to other people who wrote operas with far more notes than his own.

Salieri (1750-1825)

Although practically nothing that Salieri wrote is played today, it could be said if you had a nasty mind that his influence on European music went far beyond his capacities as a composer.

Salieri came into the family inheritance after both his parents died rather suddenly. He was looked after by the next-door neighbours who took him to Venice where he was taken up by Gassmann the Court composer. Gassmann helped Salieri to get his first opera produced, but died soon after when he unaccountably fell out of a moving carriage. Salieri took over his job and hoped he would also become Court conductor but this job was given to one Giuseppe Bonno. Bonno died rather suddenly in

1788 and Salieri eventually got the post, ultimately being appointed Director of Opera, a title which he held against all comers for a record 24 years.

In Paris, in 1787, he went to see Gluck who held several influential posts there. Gluck remarked, half-jokingly, 'I may be writing to you from Heaven very soon'; he died four days later. The place to be in those days was Vienna, and Salieri and his operas did very well there until pushed out of the opera houses by the growing success of Mozart. In 1791 Mozart died at a sadly early age, letting it be known before he expired that he thought he was being poisoned by Salieri. This was quickly hushed up as Salieri was a powerful and influential figure who taught at the Academy and held several important conducting posts. Perhaps the only person who had a greater reputation was Beethoven with whom Salieri struck up a friendship. It would be wrong to suggest that Beethoven's increasing dropsy and deafness had any connection with this. However, one of Salieri's best pupils was Schubert whom Salieri made sure didn't get a job in any opera house by recommending him (as his teacher) then turning him down (as chairman of the board).

Salieri's deathbed confessions as to the truth of all this were dismissed as the ramblings of a barmy old man.

DEATH NOTES

Death in opera is manifest in a multitude of weird guises and a knowledge of some of the more curious can provide an invaluable aid for the bluffer cornered in the bar at the interval.

Composers delight in subjecting their heroines to the most hideous tortures and bizarre terminations. Catalani's *La Wally* lives up to her name by getting swept away in an unseasonable avalanche. Selika, Meyerbeer's *L'Africaine* sits staunchly under a poisoned tree and sings an aria before expiring; Rachel, Halévy's *La Juive* is plunged into a vat of boiling oil; Janáček's *Cunning Little Vixen* gets shot by a baritone poacher, only to be subjected to the worse indignity of having her tail snipped off to make a muff.

Giordano's *Fedora* succumbs to a doctored cup of tea. Verdi's *Luisa Miller* is poisoned by a jug of lemonade. Delibes' *Lakmé* deliberately brews herself a fatal infusion of datura leaves. But these seem tame when compared to the carnal mayhem exacted by Poulenc in *Dialogues of the Carmelites* where an entire conventful of nuns is guillotined. Offenbach's revenge on Antonia in *Tales of Hoffmann* is perhaps sweetest and simplest. She just sings herself to death. Bluffers must note that it's tasteless to express a wish that other sopranos would follow her pioneering example.

And the men do not get away scot-free. Apart from earthquakes and volcanic eruptions (*Les Indes Galantes* and *The Violins of Saint-Jacques*) and the extinction of the entire human race, including tenors, in Blomdahl's *Aniara*, you need only point to the sad case of the Emperor in *The Woman without a Shadow*, who is turned, very slowly, to stone. It is rumoured that audiences at this opera are apt to share the same fate.

SOME GOOD QUOTES:

'Nothing should be sung that is necessary for the comprehension of the play.'

Corneille

'Leave your reason at home and take only your ears with you when you go to an opera house.'

Gotsched

'The Opéra is nothing but a public gathering place, where we assemble on certain days without precisely knowing why.'

Voltaire

'An exotic and irrational entertainment.'

Johnson

'In opera there is always too much singing.'

Debussy

'People are wrong when they say that opera is not what it used to be. It is what it used to be. That's what is wrong with it.'

Noël Coward

'I have often wondered whether its creator would not have paused after the first experimental effort if he could have foreseen the incredible amount of trouble he was bringing into the world.'

Beecham

'I don't mind what language an opera is sung in as long as it is a language I don't understand.'

Appleton

GLOSSARY

Alto – to come to a sudden, and usually unexpected, stop

Aria – the bits where they sing a tune

Arioso – the bits where they sing a good tune

Auftrittslied – signature tune

Ballad opera -an opera that utilises other people's tunes

Barcarolle – a song sung while rolling about in a bark

Bass – a brand of beer much sought after by baritones

Bel canto – used to mean beautiful singing; now more specifically applied to singing in which the words can't be distinguished

Brindisi – song during which the singers can have a drink

Cabaletta – taxi to and from the opera house

Casta diva – the perfect cast (rarely used)

Chamber opera – opera intended for a small number of listeners

Chest notes – music pinned to the front of a singing partner as an aide memoire

Chorus – those unable to get a decent part in the present production

Coloratura – one who messes about, adds unwanted notes

Fioritura – the actual messing about and unwanted notes involved above

Head notes – music written very small on the forehead of a singing partner as an aide memoire

Heldentenor – the chap who gets all the leading parts in operatic societies

Ho-jo-to-ho – what sopranos say on being given the part of Brünnhilde

Intermezzo – soprano who is neither one thing nor the other

Interval – the enjoyable bit of an opera

La ci darem la mano – an encouragement to applaud, literally, let's give 'em a big hand

Mad scene – the bit where everything goes wrong

Mezza voce – cut it down a bit

Milan – area surrounding La Scala

Recitative – the bits in the libretto that it didn't seem worth writing a tune for

Tenuto – notes held rather longer than is desirable

Tessitura – the range of notes in an aria that lie just beyond the capacity of the person who is supposed to sing them

Verismo – term used by Mascagni, Leoncavallo, Giordano, Puccini, Zandonai and so on, to slyly suggest that their operas were truer to life. They weren't really, though they were more lifelike than anything up to then – which isn't saying much.

C′ – the first C above the stave
C″ – the next one after that

THE AUTHOR

Peter Gammond's first introduction to opera came whe
he bought a small 7" disc with a red label in Woolworth
in 1930. It was entitled 'Ding-dong-ding-dong-ding-don;
from an operetta called *Les Cloches de Corneville*. H
never really managed to overcome its effects and ha
continued to have bad taste.

At school he appeared in opera in almost minuscular
minor roles; at university he wrote an operetta *Love an
Learning* produced with a scintillating cast of late
cabinet ministers, which was turned down by severa
leading London impresarios on the entirely justifiabl
grounds that it was no good. From that point his operati
career has proceeded in leaps and even more leaps, most o
them in the wrong direction.

Author of several well-illustrated books on opera whic
sell because of the pictures, and a number of serious work
on music, both classical and popular – some 40 books in a
– he is still slightly taken aback, when being introduced
by the instant enquiry 'Not the Gammond who wrot
Bluffer's Guide to Music?' He will never admit that he is

THE BLUFFER'S GUIDES

Available at £1.95 and (new editions) £1.99 each

Accountancy
Advertising
Antiques
Archaeology
Ballet
Bird Watching
Bluffing
British Class
The Classics
Computers
Consultancy
Cricket
EEC
Espionage
Feminism
Finance
Fortune Telling
Golf
The Green Bluffer's Guide
Hi-Fi
Hollywood
Japan
Jazz
Journalism
Literature
Management

Marketing
Maths
Modern Art
Motoring
Music
The Occult
Opera
Paris
Philosophy
Photography
Poetry
PR
Public Speaking
Publishing
Racing
Seduction
Sex
Teaching
Television
Theatre
Top Secretaries
University
Weather Forecasting
Whisky
Wine
World Affairs

All these books are available at your local bookshop or newsagent, or can be ordered direct from the publisher. Just tick the titles you require. Prices and availability subject to change without notice.

Ravette Books Limited, 3 Glenside Estate, Star Road, Partridge Green, Horsham, West Sussex RH13 8RA.

Please send a cheque or postal order, and allow the following for postage and packing: UK 25p for one book and 10p for each additional book ordered.